IS FIVE

FIVE BOOKS

by E. E. Cummings

1. The Enormous Room
2. Tulips and Chimneys
3. &
4. Xli Poems
5. Is Five

by E. E. Cummings

LIVERIGHT

NEW YORK

LIVERIGHT PUBLISHING CORPORATION

LIVERIGHT PAPERBOUND EDITION 1970

ISBN: 0-87140-002-2 (paper)
Library of Congress Catalog Card Number 76-114376
1.9876543

Printed in the United States of America

FOREWORD

On the assumption that my technique is either complicated or original or both, the publishers have politely requested me to write an introduction to this book.

At least my theory of technique, if I have one, is very far from original; nor is it complicated. I can express it in fifteen words, by quoting The Eternal Question And Immortal Answer of burlesk,viz. "Would you hit a woman with a child? —No, I'd hit her with a brick." Like the burlesk comedian, I am abnormally fond of that precision which creates movement.

If a poet is anybody, he is somebody to whom things made matter very little—somebody who is obsessed by Making. Like all obsessions, the Making obsession has disadvantages; for instance, my only interest in making money would be to make it. Fortunately, however, I should prefer to make almost anything else, including locomotives and roses. It is with roses and locomotives (not to mention acrobats Spring electricity Coney Island the 4th of July the eyes of mice and Niagara Falls) that my "poems" are competing.

They are also competing with each other, with elephants, and with El Greco.

Ineluctable preoccupation with The Verb gives a poet one priceless advantage: whereas nonmakers must content themselves with the merely undeniable fact that two times two is four, he rejoices in a purely irresistible truth (to be found, in abbreviated costume, upon the title page of the present volume.)

E. E. Cummings.

A LIST OF WHERE
THESE POEMS
have been published

*

England France Italy
Austria and
America

*

ONE

ONE
I

FIVE AMERICANS

I. LIZ

with breathing as (faithfully) her lownecked
dress a little topples and slightly expands

one square foot mired in silk wrinkling loth
stocking begins queerly to do a few
gestures to death,
                                        the silent shoulders are both
slowly with pinkish ponderous arms bedecked
whose white thick wrists deliver promptly to
a deep lap enormous mindless hands.
and no one knows what (i am sure of this)
her blunt unslender, what her big unkeen

"Business is rotten" the face yawning said

what her mouth thinks of
                                                    (if it were a kiss
distinct entirely melting sinuous lean . . .
whereof this lady in some book had read

II. MAME

ONE I

she puts down the handmirror. "Look at" arranging
before me a mellifluous idiot grin
(with what was nose upwrinkled into nothing
earthly, while the slippery eyes drown
in surging flesh). A thumblike index down-
dragging yanks back skin "see" (i, seeing, ceased
to breathe). The plump left fist opening
"wisdom." Flicker of gold. "Yep. No gas. Flynn"

the words drizzle untidily from released
cheeks "I'll tell duh woild; some noive all right.
Aint much on looks but how dat baby ached."

and when i timidly hinted "novocaine?"
the eyes outstart, curl, bloat, are newly baked

and swaggering cookies of indignant light

ONE
I

joggle i think will do it although the glad
monosyllable jounce possibly can tell
better how the balloons move (as
her ghost lurks, a Beau Brummel sticking in its three-

cornered always moist mouth)—jazz,
for whose twitching lips, between you and me
almost succeeds while toddle rings the bell.
But if her tall corpsecoloured body seat
itself (with the uncouth habitual dull
jerk at garters) there's no sharpest neat
word for the thing.
                                        Her voice?
                                                            gruesome: a trull
leaps from the lungs "gimme uh swell fite

like up ter yknow, Rektuz, Toysday nite;
where uh guy gets gayn troze uh lobstersalad

ONE
I

"life?
Listen" the feline she with radishred
legs said (crossing them slowly) "I'm
asleep. Yep. Youse is asleep kid
and everybody is." And i hazarded
"god" (blushing slightly)—"O damn
ginks like dis Gawd" opening slowlyslowly
them—then carefully the rolypoly
voice squatting on a mountain of gum did
something like a whisper, "even her."
"The Madam?" I emitted; vaguely watching
that mountainous worthy in the fragile act
of doing her eyebrows.—Marj's laughter smacked
me: pummeling the curtains, drooped to a purr . . .

i left her permanently smiling

ONE
I

should i entirely ask of god why
on the alert neck of this brittle whore
delicately wobbles an improbably distinct face,
and how these wooden big two feet conclude
happeningly the unfirm drooping bloated
calves
        i would receive the answer more
or less deserved, Young fellow go in peace.
which i do, being as Dick Mid once noted
lifting a Green River (here's to youse)
"a bloke wot's well behaved" . . . and always try
to not wonder how let's say elation
causes the bent eyes thickly to protrude—

or why her tiniest whispered invitation
is like a clock striking in a dark house

POEM, OR BEAUTY HURTS MR. VINAL

ONE
II

take it from me kiddo
believe me
my country, 'tis of

you, land of the Cluett
Shirt Boston Garter and Spearmint
Girl With The Wrigley Eyes(of you
land of the Arrow Ide
and Earl &
Wilson
Collars) of you i
sing: land of Abraham Lincoln and Lydia E. Pinkham,
land above all of Just Add Hot Water And Serve—
from every B. V. D.

let freedom ring

amen. i do however protest, anent the un
-spontaneous and otherwise scented merde which
greets one (Everywhere Why) as divine poesy per
that and this radically defunct periodical, i would

suggest that certain ideas gestures
rhymes, like Gillette Razor Blades
having been used and reused
to the mystical moment of dullness emphatically are
Not To Be Resharpened. (Case in point

if we are to believe these gently O sweetly
melancholy trillers amid the thrillers
these crepuscular violinists among my and your
skyscrapers—Helen & Cleopatra were Just Too Lovely,

direct & biting but not pessimistic

The Snail's On The Thorn enter Morn and God's
In His andsoforth

ONE
II

do you get me?)according
to such supposedly indigenous
throstles Art is O World O Life
a formula: example, Turn Your Shirttails Into
Drawers and If It Isn't An Eastman It Isn't A
Kodak therefore my friends let
us now sing each and all fortissimo A-
mer
i

ca, I
love,
You. And there're a
hun-dred-mil-lion-oth-ers, like
all of you successfully if
delicately gelded(or spaded)
gentlemen(and ladies)—pretty

conformists

littleliverpill-
hearted-Nujolneeding-There's-A-Reason
americans(who tensetendoned and with
upward vacant eyes, painfully
perpetually crouched, quivering, upon the
sternly allotted sandpile
—how silently
emit a tiny violetflavoured nuisance: Odor?

human excrement!

ono.
comes out like a ribbon lies flat on the brush

curtains part)
the peacockappareled
prodigy of Flo''s midnight
Frolic dolores

small in the head keen chassised like a Rolls
Royce
swoopssmoothly
                    outward(amid
tinkling-cheering-hammering

tables)

while softly along Kirkland Street
the infantile ghost of Professor
Royce rolls

remembering that it

has for
-gotten some-
thing ah

(my

necktie

workingman with hand so hairy-sturdy
you may turn O turn that airy hurdysturdygurdy
but when will turn backward O backward Time in your no thy flight
and make me a child, a pretty dribbling child, a little child.

In thy your ear:
en amerique on ne boit que de Jingyale.
things are going rather kaka
over there, over there.
yet we scarcely fare much better—

what's become of (if you please)
all the glory that or which was Greece
all the grandja
that was dada?

make me a child, stout hurdysturdygurdyman
waiter, make me a child. So this is Paris.
i will sit in the corner and drink thinks and think drinks,
in memory of the Grand and Old days:
of Amy Sandburg
of Algernon Carl Swinburned.

Waiter a drink waiter two or three drinks
what's become of Mæterlink
now that April's here?
(ask the man who owns one
ask Dad, He knows).

ONE
V

yonder deadfromtheneckup graduate of a
somewhat obscure to be sure university spends
her time looking picturesque under

the as it happens quite
erroneous impression that he

nascitur

ONE
VI

Jimmie's got a goil
goil
goil,
Jimmie
's got a goil and
she coitnly can shimmie — urban lingo

when you see her shake
shake
shake,
when
you see her shake a
shimmie how you wish that you was Jimmie.

Oh for such a gurl
gurl
gurl,
oh
for such a gurl to
be a fellow's twistandtwirl

talk about your Sal-
Sal-
Sal-,
talk
about your Salo
-mes but gimmie Jimmie's gal.

? chanting, part of that school boy "gang mentality" which C. so opposed — influenced his devotion to individualism

ONE
VII

the waddling
madam star
taps
taps. “ready girls”. the

unspontaneous streets
make bright their eyes
a
blind irisher fiddles a

scotch jig in a stinking
joyman bar
a cockney is
buying whiskies for a turk

a waiter ıntones:bloo-moo-n
sirkusricky
platzburg
hoppytoad yesmam. the

furious taximan
p(ee)ps
on his whistle somebody
says here’s luck

somebody else says down the hatch
the nigger smiles
the jew stands
besides his teddy-bears

the sailor shuffles the
night with ϕυκινγ eyes
the great black preacher gargles jesus
the aesthete indulges

his soul for certain things which died
it is eighteen hundred
years....
exactly

 under the window
 under the window
 under the window walk

the unburied feet of
the little ladies more than dead

ONE
VIII

listen my children and you
shall hear the true

story of Mr Do
-nothing the wellknown parvenu
who

(having dreamed of a corkscrew)
studied with Freud a year or two
and when Freud got through
with Do-

nothing Do
-nothing could do
nothing which you
and i are accustomed to
accomplish two

or three times, and even a few
more depending on the remu-
nerativeness of the stimulus(eheu
fu
-gaces Postu-
me boo

who)

even if all desires things moments be ONE
murderedknownphotographed,ourselvesyawningwillaskourselves
ou sont les neiges. . . . some IX

guys talks big

about Lundun Burlin an gay Paree an
some guys claims der never was
nutn like Nooer Leans Shikahgo Sain
Looey Noo York an San Fran dictaphones
wireless subways vacuum
cleaners pianolas funnygraphs skyscrapers an safetyrazors

sall right in its way kiddo
but as fer i gimme de good ole daze. . . .

in dem daze kid Christmas
meant sumpn youse knows wot
i refers ter Satter Nailyuh(comes but once er
year)i'll tell de woild one swell bangup
time wen nobody wore no cloze
an went runnin aroun wid eachudder Hell
Bent fer election makin believe dey was chust born

ONE
X

death is more than
certain a hundred these
sounds crowds odours it
is in a hurry
beyond that any this
taxi smile or angle we do

not sell and buy
things so necessary as
is death and unlike shirts
neckties trousers
we cannot wear it out

no sir which is why
granted who discovered
America ether the movies
may claim general importance

to me to you nothing is
what particularly
matters hence in a

little sunlight and less
moonlight ourselves against the worms

hate laugh shimmy

nobody loses all the time

i had an uncle named
Sol who was a born failure and
nearly everybody said he should have gone
into vaudeville perhaps because my Uncle Sol could
sing McCann He Was A Diver on Xmas Eve like Hell Itself which
may or may not account for the fact that my Uncle

Sol indulged in that possibly most inexcusable
of all to use a highfalootin phrase
luxuries that is or to
wit farming and be
it needlessly
added

my Uncle Sol's farm
failed because the chickens
ate the vegetables so
my Uncle Sol had a
chicken farm till the
skunks ate the chickens when

my Uncle Sol
had a skunk farm but
the skunks caught cold and
died and so
my Uncle Sol imitated the
skunks in a subtle manner

or by drowning himself in the watertank
but somebody who'd given my Uncle Sol a Victor
Victrola and records while he lived presented to
him upon the auspicious occasion of his decease a

ONE
XI

scrumptious not to mention splendiferous funeral with
tall boys in black gloves and flowers and everything and

i remember we all cried like the Missouri
when my Uncle Sol's coffin lurched because
somebody pressed a button
(and down went
my Uncle
Sol

and started a worm farm)

ONE
XII

now dis "daughter" uv eve(who aint precisely slim)sim

ply don't know duh meanin uv duh woid sin in
not disagreeable contras tuh dat not exacly fat

"father"(adjustin his robe)who now puts on his flat hat

ONE
XIII

(and i imagine
never mind Joe agreeably cheerfully remarked when
surrounded by fat stupid animals
the jewess shrieked
the messiah tumbled successfully into the world
the animals continued eating. And i imagine she, and
heard them slobber and
in the darkness)

stood sharp angels with faces like Jim Europe

ONE
XIV

it really must
be Nice, never to

have no imagination)or never
never to wonder about guys you used to(and them
slim hot queens with dam next to nothing

on)tangoing
(while a feller tries
to hold down the fifty bucks per
job with one foot and rock a

cradle with the other)it Must be
nice never to have no doubts about why you
put the ring
on(and watching her
face grow old and tired to which

you're married and hands get red washing
things and dishes)and to never, never really wonder i
mean about the smell
of babies and how you

know the dam rent's going to and everything and never, never
Never to stand at no window
because i can't sleep(smoking sawdust

cigarettes in the
middle of the night

Bemoaning the nature of life itself

the more thinking or intelligent a person is the more unrest he feels, the more worries he has. "It must be nice" to be dull and mindless and oblivious to it all.

ONE
XV

this man is o so
Waiter
this;woman is

please shut that
the pout And affectionate leer
interminable pyramidal,napkins
(this man is oh so tired of this
a door opens by itself
woman.) they so to speak were in

Love once?
now
her mouth opens too far
and:she attacks her Lobster without
feet mingle under the
mercy.
(exit the hors d'œuvres)

ONE
XVI

it started when Bill's chip let on to
the bulls he'd bumped a bloke back in fifteen.
Then she came toward him on her knees across the locked
room.   he knocked her cold and beat it for Chicago.

Eddie was waiting for him, and they cleaned up a few
times—before she got the info
from a broad that knew Eddie in Topeka, went clean
daffy, and which was very silly hocked

the diamond he gave her.   Bill was put wise
that she was coming with his kid inside her.
He laughed. She came. he gave her a shove
and asked Eddie did he care to ride her?
. . . . she exactly lay, looking hunks of love

in The Chair he kept talking about eyes

we have only the essential elements of
the story
a ballad
the distruction of Bill

ONE
XVII

IKEY(GOLDBERG)'S WORTH I'M
TOLD $ SEVERAL MILLION
FINKLESTEIN(FRITZ)LIVES
AT THE RITZ WEAR
earl & wilson COLLARS

?

ONE
XVIII

why are these pipples taking their hets off?
the king & queen
alighting from their limousine
inhabit the Hotel Meurice (whereas
i live in a garret and eat aspirine)

but who is this pale softish almost round
young man to whom headwaiters bow so?
hush—the author of Women By Night whose latest Seeds
Of Evil sold 69 carloads before
publication the girl who goes wrong you

know (whereas when i lie down i cough too
much). How did the traffic get so jammed?
bedad it is the famous doctor who inserts
monkeyglands in millionaires a cute idea n'est-ce pas?
(whereas, upon the other hand, myself) but let us next demand

wherefore yon mob
an accident? somebody got concus-
sion of the brain?—Not
a bit of it, my dears merely the prime
minister of Siam in native

costume, who
emerging from a pissoir
enters abruptly Notre Dame (whereas
de gustibus non disputandum est
my lady is tired of That sort of thing

ONE
XIX

this young question mark man

question mark
who suffers from
indigestion question
mark is a remarkably
charming person

personally they tell

me as for me
i only knows that
as far as
his pictures goes

he's a wet dream

by Cézanne

mr youse needn't be so spry
concernin questions arty

each has his tastes but as for i
i likes a certain party

gimme the he-man's solid bliss
for youse ideas i'll match youse

a pretty girl who naked is
is worth a million statues

ONE XXI

i was sitting in mcsorley's. outside it was New York and beatifully snowing.

Inside snug and evil. the slobbering walls filthily push witless creases of screaming warmth chuck pillows are noise funnily swallows swallowing revolvingly pompous a the swallowed mottle with smooth or a but of rapidly goes gobs the and of flecks of and a chatter sobbings intersect with which distinct disks of graceful oath, upsoarings the break on ceiling-flatness

the Bar.tinking luscious jigs dint of ripe silver with warmlyish wetflat splurging smells waltz the glush of squirting taps plus slush of foam knocked off and a faint piddle-of-drops she says I ploc spittle what the lands thaz me kid in no sir hopping sawdust you kiddo he's a palping wreaths of badly Yep cigars who jim him why gluey grins topple together eyes pout gestures stickily point made glints squinting who's a wink bum-nothing and money fuzzily mouths take big wobbly foot-steps every goggle cent of it get out ears dribbles soft right old feller belch the chap hic summore eh chuckles skulch . . . .

and i was sitting in the din thinking drinking the ale, which never lets you grow old blinking at the low ceiling my being pleasantly was punctuated by the always retchings of a worthless lamp.

when With a minute terrif iceffort one dirty squeal of soiling light yanKing from bushy obscurity a bald greenish foetal head established It suddenly upon the

huge neck around whose unwashed sonorous muscle
the filth of a collar hung gently.

(spattered)by this instant of semiluminous nausea A
vast wordless nondescript genie of trunk trickled firm-
ly in to one exactly-mutilated ghost of a chair,

a;domeshaped interval of complete plasticity,shoul-
ders,sprouted the extraordinary arms through an an-
gle of ridiculous velocity commenting upon an un-
clean table.and,whose distended immense Both paws
slowly loved a dinted mug

gone Darkness   it was so near to me,i ask of shad-
ow won't you have a drink?

(the eternal perpetual question)

Inside snugandevil.   i was sitting in mcsorley's
It,did not answer.

outside.(it was New York and beautifully,snowing....

ONE
XXII

she being Brand

-new;and you
know consequently a
little stiff i was
careful of her and(having

thoroughly oiled the universal
joint tested my gas felt of
her radiator made sure her springs were O.

K.)i went right to it flooded-the-carburetor cranked her

up,slipped the
clutch(and then somehow got into reverse she
kicked what
the hell)next
minute i was back in neutral tried and

again slo-wly;bare,ly nudg.   ing(my

lev-er Right-
oh and her gears being in
A 1 shape passed
from low through
second-in-to-high like
greasedlightning just as we turned the corner of Divinity

avenue i touched the accelerator and give

her the juice,good

(it

ONE
XXII

was the first ride and believe i we was
happy to see how nice she acted right up to
the last minute coming back down by the Public
Gardens i slammed on
the

internalexpanding
&
externalcontracting
brakes Bothatonce and

brought allofher tremB
-ling
to a:dead.

stand-
;Still)

ONE
XXIII

slightly before the middle of Congressman Pudd
's 4th of July oration, with a curse and a frown
Amy Lowell got up
and all the little schoolchildren sat down

ONE
XXIV

Dick Mid's large bluish face without eyebrows

sits in the kitchen nights and chews a two-bit cigar
waiting for the bulls to pull his joint.
Jimmie was a dude. Dark hair and nice hands.

with a little eye that rolled and made its point

Jimmie's sister worked for Dick. And had some rows
over percent. The gang got shot up twice, it
operated in the hundred ands

All the chips would kid Jimmie to give them a kiss
but Jimmie lived regular. stewed three times a week.
and slept twice a week with a big toothless girl
in Yonkers.
Dick Mid's green large three teeth leak

smoke: remembering, two pink big lips curl . . . .

how Jimmie was framed and got his

oDE

ONE
XXV

o

the sweet & aged people
who rule this world(and me and
you if we're not very
careful)

O,

the darling benevolent mindless
He—and She—
shaped waxworks filled
with dead ideas(the oh

quintillions of incredible
dodderingly godly toothless
always-so-much-interested-
in-everybody-else's-business

bipeds)OH
the bothering
dear unnecessary hairless
o

ld

on the Madam's best april the
twenty nellie

anyway and
it's flutters everything
queer;does smells he smiles is
like Out of doors he's a with
eyes and making twice the a week
you kind of,know(kind well of
A sort of the way he smile but
and her a I mean me a
Irish,cook but well oh don't
you makes burst want to dear somehow
quickyes when(now,dark dear oh)
the iceman
how,luminously
oh how listens and,expands
my somewhereallover me heart my
the halfgloom coolish
of The what are
parks for wiggle yes has
are leap,which,anyway

give rapid lapfulls of
idiotic big hands

ONE
XXVII

(as that named Fred
-someBody: hippopotamus, scratch-
ing,one,knee with,its,
friend observes I

pass Mr Tom Larsen twirls among

pale lips the extinct
cigar)at

which

this(once flinger
of lariats lean exroper of
horned suddenly crashing things)man spits

quickly into the very bright spittoon

ONE
XXVIII

my uncle
Daniel fought in the civil
war band and can play the triangle
like the devil)my

uncle Frank has done nothing for many
years but fly kites and
when the
string breaks(or something)my uncle Frank breaks into
tears.   my uncle Tom

knits and is a kewpie above the ears(but

my uncle Ed
that's
dead from the neck

up is lead all over
Brattle Street by a castrated pup

than(by yon sunset's wintry glow
revealed)this tall strong stalwart youth,
what sight shall human optics know
more quite ennobling forsooth?

One wondrous fine sonofabitch
(to all purposes and intents)
in which distinct and rich
portrait should be included,gents

these(by the fire's ruddy glow
united)not less than sixteen
children and of course you know
their mother,of his heart the queen

—incalculable bliss!
Picture it gents: our hero,Dan
who as you've guessed already is
the poorbuthonest workingman

(by that bright flame whose myriad tints
enrich a visage simple,terse,
seated like any king or prince
upon his uncorrupted arse

with all his hearty soul aglow)
his nightly supper sups
it isn't snowing snow you know
it's snowing buttercups

ONE
XXX

weazened Irrefutable unastonished
two, countenances seated in arranging; sunlight
with-ered unspea-king: tWeNtY, f i n g e r s , large
four gnarled lips totter

Therefore, approaching my twentysix selves
bulging in immortal Spring express a cry of
How do you find the sun, ladies?

(graduallyverygradually "there is not enough
of it" their, hands
minutely

answered

ONE
XXXI

stop look &

listen Venezia: incline thine
ear you glassworks
of Murano;
pause
elevator nel
mezzo del cammin' that means half-
way up the Campanile, believe

thou me cocodrillo—

mine eyes have seen
the glory of

the coming of
the Americans particularly the
brand of marriageable nymph which is
armed with large legs rancid
voices Baedekers Mothers and kodaks
—by night upon the Riva Schiavoni or in
the felicitous vicinity of the de l'Europe

Grand and Royal
Danielli their numbers

are like unto the stars of Heaven. . . .

i do signore
affirm that all gondola signore
day below me gondola signore gondola
and above me pass loudly and gondola

rapidly denizens of Omaha Altoona or what
not enthusiastic cohorts from Duluth God only,
gondola knows Cincingondolanati i gondola don't

—the substantial dollarbringing virgins

"from the Loggia where
are we angels by O yes
beautiful we now pass through the look
girls in the style of that's the
foliage what is it didn't Ruskin
says about you got the haven't Marjorie
isn't this wellcurb simply darling"
—O Education:O
thos cook & son

(O to be a metope
now that triglyph's here)

ONE
XXXII

a man who had fallen among thieves
lay by the roadside on his back
dressed in fifteenthrate ideas
wearing a round jeer for a hat

fate per a somewhat more than less
emancipated evening
had in return for consciousness
endowed him with a changeless grin

whereon a dozen staunch and leal
citizens did graze at pause
then fired by hypercivic zeal
sought newer pastures or because

swaddled with a frozen brook
of pinkest vomit out of eyes
which noticed nobody he looked
as if he did not care to rise

one hand did nothing on the vest
its wideflung friend clenched weakly dirt
while the mute trouserfly confessed
a button solemnly inert.

Brushing from whom the stiffened puke
i put him all into my arms
and staggered banged with terror through
a million billion trillion stars

ONE
XXXIII

Babylon slim
-ness of
evenslicing
eyes are chisels

scarlet Goes
with her
whitehot
face,gashed

by hair's blue cold

jolts of
lovecrazed abrupt

flesh split "Pretty
Baby"
to
numb rhythm before christ

ONE
XXXIV

this evangelist
buttons with his big gollywog voice
the kingdomofheaven up behind and crazily
skating thither and hither in filthy sawdust
chucks and rolls
against the tent his thick joggling fists

he is persuasive

the editor cigarstinking hobgoblin swims
upwardinhisswivelchaironefistdanglingscandalwhile
five other fingers snitch
rapidly through mist a defunct king as

linotypes gobblehobble

our lightheavy twic twoc ingly attacks
landing a onetwo
which doubles up suddenly his bunged hinging
victim against the
giving ropes amid
screams of deeply bulging thousands

i too omit one kelly

in response to howjedooze the candidate's new silk
lid bounds gently from his baldness
a smile masturbates softly in the vacant
lot of his physiognomy
his scientifically pressed trousers ejaculate spats

a strikingly succulent getup

but
we knew a muffhunter and he said to us Kid.
daze nutn like it.

ONE
XXXV

(ponder,darling,these busted statues
of yon motheaten forum be aware
notice what hath remained
—the stone cringes
clinging to the stone,how obsolete

lips utter their extant smile . . . .
remark

a few deleted of texture
or meaning monuments and dolls

resist Them Greediest Paws of careful
time all of which is extremely
unimportant)whereas Life

matters if or

when the your- and my-
idle vertical worthless
self unite in a peculiarly
momentary

partnership(to instigate
constructive
                Horizontal
business . . . . even so,let us make haste
—consider well this ruined aqueduct

lady,
which used to lead something into somewhere)

ONE
XXXVI

ta
ppin
g
toe

hip
popot
amus Back

gen
teel-ly
lugu-
bri ous

                    eyes
LOOPTHELOOP

as

fathandsbangrag

poets yeggs and thirsties

ONE XXXVII

since we are spanked and put to sleep by dolls let
us not be continually astonished should
from their actions and speeches
sawdust perpetually leak

rather is it between such beddings and
bumpings of ourselves to be observed
how in this fundamental respect the well
recognised regime of childhood is reversed

meantime in dreams let us investigate
thoroughly each one his optima rerum first
having taken care to lie upon our
abdomens for greater privacy and lest

punished bottoms interrupt philosophy

ONE XXXVIII

Will i ever forget that precarious moment?

As i was standing on the third rail waiting for the next train to grind me into lifeless atoms various absurd thoughts slyly crept into my highly sexed mind.

It seemed to me that i had first of all really made quite a mistake in being at all born, seeing that i was wifeless and only half awake, cursed with pimples, correctly dressed, cleanshaven above the nombril, and much to my astonishment much impressed by having once noticed (as an infantile phenomenon) George Washington almost incompletely surrounded by well-drawn icecakes beheld being too strong, in brief : an American, if you understand that i mean what i say i believe my most intimate friends would never have gathered.

A collarbutton which had always not nothurt me not much and in the same place.

Why according to tomorrow's paper the proletariat will not rise yesterday.

Inexpressible itchings to be photographed with Lord Rothermere playing with Lord Rothermere billiards very well by moonlight with Lord Rothermere.

A crockodile eats a native, who in revenge beats it insensible with a banana, establishing meanwhile a religious cult based on consubstantial intangibility.

 Personne ne m'aime et j'ai les mains froides.

His Royal Highness said "peek-a-boo" and thirty tame fleas left the prettily embroidered howdah immediately.

Thumbprints of an angel named Frederick found on a lightning-rod, Boston, Mass.

such were the not unhurried reflections to which my organ of imperception gave birth to which i should ordinarily have objected to which, considering the background, it is hardly surprising if anyone hardly should call exactly extraordinary. We refer, of course, to my position. A bachelor incapable of occupation, he had long suppressed the desire to suppress the suppressed desire of shall we say: Idleness, while meaning its opposite? Nothing could be clearer to all concerned than that i am not a policeman.

Meanwhile the tea regressed.

Kipling again H. G. Wells, and Anatole France shook hands again and yet again shook again hands again, the former coachman with a pipewrench of the again latter then opening a box of newly without exaggeration shot with some difficulty sardines. Mr. Wiggin took Wrs. Miggin's harm in is, extinguishing the spitoon by a candle furnished by courtesy of the management on Thursdays, opposite which a church stood perfectly upright but not piano item:a watermelon causes indigestion to William Cullen Longfellow's small negro son, Henry Wadsworth Bryant.

By this time, however, the flight of crows had ceased. I withdrew my hands from the tennisracket. All was over. One brief convulsive octopus, and then our hero folded his umbrella.

It seemed too beautiful.

Let us perhaps excuse me if i repeat himself: these, or nearly these, were the not unpainful thoughts which occupied the subject of our attention; to speak even less objectively, i was horribly scared i would actually fall off the rail before the really train after all arrived. If i should have made this perfectly clear, it entirely would have been not my fault.

voices to voices, lip to lip
i swear (to noone everyone) constitutes
undying; or whatever this and that petal confutes . . .
to exist being a peculiar form of sleep

what's beyond logic happens beneath will;
nor can these moments be translated: i say
that even after April
by God there is no excuse for May

—bring forth your flowers and machinery: sculpture and prose
flowers guess and miss
machinery is the more accurate, yes
it delivers the goods, Heaven knows

(yet are we mindful, though not as yet awake,
of ourselves which shout and cling, being
for a little while and which easily break
in spite of the best overseeing)

i mean that the blond absence of any program
except last and always and first to live
makes unimportant what i and you believe;
not for philosophy does this rose give a damn . . .

bring on your fireworks, which are a mixed
splendor of piston and of pistil; very well
provided an instant may be fixed
so that it will not rub, like any other pastel.

(While you and i have lips and voices which
are for kissing and to sing with
who cares if some oneeyed son of a bitch
invents an instrument to measure Spring with?

ONE XXXIX

each dream nascitur, is not made . . .)
why then to Hell with that: the other; this,
since the thing perhaps is
to eat flowers and not to be afraid.

ONE

XL

life hurl my
yes,crumbles hand(ful released conarefetti)ev eryflitter,inga. where
mil(lions of aflickf)litter ing brightmillion ofS hurl;edindodg:ing
whom areEyes shy-dodge is bright cruMbshandful,quick-hurl edinwho
Is flittercrumbs,fluttercrimbs are floatfallin,g;allwhere:
a:crimbflitteringish is arefloatsis ingfallall!mil,shy milbrightlions
my(hurl flicker handful
in)dodging are shybrigHteyes is crum bs(alll)if,ey Es

TWO

TWO
I

the season 'tis, my lovely lambs,

of Sumner Volstead Christ and Co.
the epoch of Mann's righteousness
the age of dollars and no sense.
Which being quite beyond dispute

as prove from Troy (N. Y.) to Cairo
(Egypt) the luminous dithyrambs
of large immaculate unmute
antibolshevistic gents
(each manufacturing word by word
his own unrivalled brand of pyro
-technic blurb anent the (hic)
hero dead that gladly (sic)
in far lands perished of unheard
of maladies including flu)

my little darlings, let us now
passionately remember how—
braving the worst, of peril heedless,
each braver than the other, each
(a typewriter within his reach)
upon his fearless derrière
sturdily seated—Colonel Needless
To Name and General You know who
a string of pretty medals drew

(while messrs jack james john and jim
in token of their country's love
received my dears the order of
The Artificial Arm and Limb)

—or, since bloodshed and kindred questions
inhibit unprepared digestions,

TWO
I

come: let us mildly contemplate
beginning with his wellfilled pants
earth's biggest grafter, nothing less;
the Honorable Mr. (guess)
who, breathing on the ear of fate,
landed a seat in the legislat-
ure whereas tommy so and so
(an erring child of circumstance
whom the bulls nabbed at 33rd)

pulled six months for selling snow

TWO
II

opening of the chambers close

quotes the microscopic pithicoid President
in a new frock
coat(scrambling all
up over the tribune dances crazily
& &)&
chatters about Peacepeacepeace(to
droppingly
descend amid thunderous anthropoid applause)pronounced

by the way Pay the

extremely artistic nevertobeextinguished fla
-me of the(very prettily indeed)arra-
nged souvenir of the in spite of himself fa
-mous soldier minus his na-
me(so as not to hurt the perspective of the(hei
-nous thought)otherwise immaculately tabulated vicinity)invei-
gles a few mildly curious rai
-ned on people(both male and female
created He

then,   And every beast of the field

TWO
III

"next to of course god america i
love you land of the pilgrims' and so forth oh
say can you see by the dawn's early my
country 'tis of centuries come and go
and are no more what of it we should worry
in every language even deafanddumb
thy sons acclaim your glorious name by gorry
by jingo by gee by gosh by gum
why talk of beauty what could be more beaut-
iful than these heroic happy dead
who rushed like lions to the roaring slaughter
they did not stop to think they died instead
then shall the voices of liberty be mute?"

He spoke. And drank rapidly a glass of water

endless clichés

TWO
IV

it's jolly
odd what pops into
your jolly tete when the
jolly shells begin dropping jolly fast you
hear the rrmp and
then nearerandnearerandNEARER
and before
you can

!

& we're

NOT
(oh—
—i say

that's jolly odd
old thing, jolly
odd, jolly
jolly odd isn't
it jolly odd.

TWO
V

look at this)
a 75 done
this nobody would
have believed
would they no
kidding this was my particular

pal
funny aint
it we was
buddies
i used to

know
him lift the
poor cuss
tenderly this side up handle

with care
fragile
and send him home

to his old mother in
a new nice pine box

(collect

first Jock he
was kilt a handsome
man and James and
next let me
see yes Will that was
cleverest
he was kilt and my youngest
boy was kilt last with
the big eyes i loved like you can't
imagine Harry was o
god kilt he was kilt everybody was kilt

they called them the kilties

TWO
VII

lis
-ten

you know what i mean when
the first guy drops you know
everybody feels sick or
when they throw in a few gas
and the oh baby shrapnel
or my feet getting dim freezing or
up to your you know what in water or
with the bugs crawling right all up
all everywhere over you all me everyone
that's been there knows what
i mean a god damned lot of
people don't and never
never
will know,
they don't want

to
no

a comment on those who have
never known war.

TWO
VIII

come, gaze with me upon this dome
of many coloured glass, and see
his mother's pride, his father's joy,
unto whom duty whispers low

"thou must!" and who replies "I can!"
—yon clean upstanding well dressed boy
that with his peers full oft hath quaffed
the wine of life and found it sweet—

a tear within his stern blue eye,
upon his firm white lips a smile,
one thought alone: to do or die
for God for country and for Yale

above his blond determined head
the sacred flag of truth unfurled,
in the bright heyday of his youth
the upper class American

unsullied stands, before the world:
with manly heart and conscience free,
upon the front steps of her home
by the high minded pure young girl

much kissed, by loving relatives
well fed, and fully photographed
the son of man goes forth to war
with trumpets clap and syphilis

A social satire in which Cummings emphasizes the false stereotyped ideas of war.

TWO
IX

little ladies more
than dead exactly dance
in my head, precisely
dance where danced la guerre.

Mimi a
la voix fragile
qui chatouille Des
Italiens

the putain with the ivory throat
Marie Louise Lallemand
n'es-ce pas que je suis belle
cheri? les anglais m'aiment
tous, les americains
aussi . . . . "bon dos, bon cul de Paris"(Marie
Vierge
Priez
Pour
Nous)

with the
long lips of
Lucienne which dangle
the old men and hot
men se promenent
doucement le soir(ladies

accurately dead les anglais
sont gentils et les americains
aussi, ils payent bien les americains dance

exactly in my brain voulez
vous coucher avec
moi? Non? pourquoi?

TWO
IX

ladies skilfully
dead precisely dance
where has danced la
guerre j'm'appelle
Manon, cinq rue Henri Mounier
voulez vous coucher avec moi?
te ferai Mimi
te ferai Minette,
dead exactly dance
si vous voulez
chatouiller
mon lezard ladies suddenly
j'm'en fout de negres

(in the twilight of Paris
Marie Louise with queenly
legs cinq rue Henri
Mounier a little love
begs, Mimi with the body
like une boite a joujoux, want nice sleep?
toutes les petites femmes exactes
qui dansent toujours in my
head dis-donc,Paris

ta gorge mysterieuse
pourquoi se promene-t-elle, pourquoi
eclate ta voix
fragile couleur de pivoine?)
with the

long lips of Lucienne which
dangle the old men and hot men
precisely dance in my head
ladies carefully dead

TWO
X

16 heures
l'Etoile

the communists have fine Eyes

some are young some old none
look alike the flics rush
batter the crowd sprawls collapses
singing knocked down trampled the kicked by
flics rush(the

Flics, tidiyum, are
very tidiyum reassuringly similar,
they all have very tidiyum
mustaches, and very
tidiyum chins, and just above
their very tidiyum ears their
very tidiyum necks begin)
                                        let us add

that there are 50(fifty)flics for every
one(1)communist and
all the flics are very organically
arranged
and their nucleus(composed
of captains in freshly-creased
-uniforms with only-just-
shined buttons
tidiyum
before and behind)has a nucleolus:

the Prefect of Police

(a dapper derbied

creature, swaggers daintily
twiddling
his tiny cane
and, mazurkas about tweak-
ing his wing collar pecking at his im

-peccable cravat directing being
shooting his cuffs
saluted everywhere saluting
reviewing processions of minions
tappingpeopleontheback

"allezcirculez")

—my   he's brave . . . .
the
communists pick
up themselves friends
& their hats legs &

arms brush dirt coats
smile looking hands
spit blood teeth

the Communists have(very)fine eyes
(which stroll hither and thither through the
evening in bruised narrow questioning faces)

TWO
XI

my sweet old etcetera
aunt lucy during the recent

war could and what
is more did tell you just
what everybody was fighting

for,
my sister

isabel created hundreds
(and
hundreds)of socks not to
mention shirts fleaproof earwarmers

etcetera wristers etcetera, my
mother hoped that

i would die etcetera
bravely of course my father used
to become hoarse talking about how it was
a privilege and if only he
could meanwhile my

self etcetera lay quietly
in the deep mud et

cetera
(dreaming,
et
  cetera, of
Your smile
eyes knees and of your Etcetera)

concerns the difference between the actuality of war and the idealistic views held by those who have never known war.

the soldier is the the only one who knows what war really means

Simply a statement
no bitterness against the non-soldier
only against the war itself.

THREE

THREE
I

now that fierce few
flowers(stealthily)
in the alive west
begin

requiescat this six
feet of Breton big good
body, which terminated
in fists hair wood

erect cursing hatless who
(bent by wind)slammed hard-
over the tiller;clattered
forward skidding in outrageous

sabots language trickling
pried his black
mouth with fat jibing
lips,

once upon a
(that is
over: and the sea heaving
indolent colourless forgets)time

Requiescat.
carry
carefully the blessed large silent him
into nibbling final worms

THREE
II

Among

these
red pieces of
day(against which and
quite silently hills
made of blueandgreen paper

scorchbend ingthem
-selves-U
pcurv E,into:
anguish(clim
b)ing
s-p-i-r-a-
l
and,disappear)
Satanic and blasé

a black goat lookingly wanders

There is nothing left of the world but
into this noth
ing il treno per
Roma si-gnori?
jerk.
ilyr,ushes

THREE
III

it is winter a moon in the afternoon
and warm air turning into January darkness up
through which sprouting gently, the cathedral
leans its dreamy spine against thick sunset

i perceive in front of our lady a ring of people
a brittle swoon of centrifugally expecting
faces clumsily which devours a man, three cats,
five white mice, and a baboon.

O a monkey with a sharp face waddling carefully
the length of this padded pole; a monkey attached
by a chain securely to this always talking
individual, mysterious witty hatless.

Cats which move smoothly from neck to neck of bottles, cats
smoothly willowing out and in between bottles, who step smoothly
and rapidly along this pole over five squirming
mice; or leap through hoops of fire, creating smoothness.

People stare, the drunker applaud
while twilight takes the sting out of the vermilion
jacket of nodding hairy Jaqueline who is given a mouse
to hold lovingly,

our lady what do you think of this? Do your proud fingers and
your arms tremble remembering something squirming fragile
and which had been presented unto you by a mystery?
. . . the cathedral recedes into weather without answering

THREE
IV

impossibly

motivated by midnight
the flyspecked abdominous female
indubitably tellurian
strolls
        emitting minute grins

each an intaglio.
Nothing
has also carved upon her much

too white forehead a pair of
eyes which mutter thickly(as one merely
terriculous American an instant doubts
the authenticity

of these antiquities—relaxing
                                        hurries
elsewhere;to blow

incredible wampum

THREE
V

inthe,exquisite;

morning   sure   lyHer eye s exactly sit,ata little roundtable
among otherlittle roundtables Her,eyes   count   slow(ly

obstre poroustimidi ties surElyfl)oat iNg,the

ofpieces ofof sunligh tof fa l l in gof throughof treesOf.

(Fields Elysian

the like,a)slEEping neck a breathing a   ,lies
(slo wlythe wom an pa)ris her
flesh:wakes
                    in little streets

while exactlygir lisHlegs;play;ing;nake;D
and

chairs wait under the trees

Fields slowly Elysian in
a firmcool-Ness   taxis,s.QuirM

and,   b etw ee nch air st ott er sthesillyold
WomanSellingBaloonS

In theex qui site

morning,
            her sureLyeye ssit-ex actly her sitsat a surely! little,
roundtable amongother; littleexactly round.   tables,

Her
      .eyes

THREE
VI

candles and

Here Comes a glass box
which the exhumed
hand of Saint Ignatz miraculously
inhabits. (people tumble
down. people crumble to their
knees. people
begin crossing people) and

hErE cOmEs a glass box:
surrounded by priests
moving in fifty colours
, sensuously

(the crowd
howls faintly
blubbering pointing

see
yes)
It
here
comes

A Glass
Box and incense with

and oh sunlight—
the crash of the
colours (of the oh
silently
striding) priests-and-
slowly,al,ways;procession:and

Enters

this
    church.

toward which The
Expectant stutter(upon artificial limbs,
with faces like defunct geraniums)

THREE VII

Paris;this April sunset completely utters
utters serenely silently a cathedral

before whose upward lean magnificent face
the streets turn young with rain,

spiral acres of bloated rose
coiled within cobalt miles of sky
yield to and heed
the mauve
                    of twilight(who slenderly descends,
daintily carrying in her eyes the dangerous first stars)
people move love hurry in a gently

arriving gloom and
see!(the new moon
fills abruptly with sudden silver
these torn pockets of lame and begging colour)while
there and here the lithe indolent prostitute
Night,argues

with certain houses

will out of the kindness of their hearts a few philosophers tell me
what am i doing on top of this hill at Calchidas, in the sunlight?
down ever so far on the beach below me a little girl in white spins,tumbles; rolling in sand.
across this water,crowding tints:browns and whites shoving,the dotting millions of windows of thousands of houses—Lisboa. Like the crackle of a typewriter,in the afternoon sky.
goats and sheep are driven by somebody along a curve of road which eats into a pink cliff back and up leaning out of yellowgreen water.

they are building a house down there by the sea,in the afternoon.

rapidly a reddish ant travels my fifth finger.
a bird chirps in a tree,somewhere nowhere
and a little girl in white is tumbling
in sand
Clouds over
me are like bridegrooms

Naked and luminous

(here the absurd I; life, to peer and wear clothes. i am altogether foolish, i suddenly make a fist out of ten fingers
voices rise from down ever so far—
hush.
Sunlight,
there are old men behind me I tell you; several,incredible,sleepy

THREE
IX

but observe;although
once is never the beginning of
enough, is it(i do not pretend
to know the reason any more than.)But look:up-

raising, hoisting, a little
perhaps that and this, deftly
propping on smallest hands
the slim hinging you
                                        —because
it's five o'clock

and these(i notice)trees winterbrief surly old
gurgle a nonsense of sparrows, the cathedral
shudders blackening;
the sky is washed with tone

now for a moon
to squat in first darkness
—a little moon thinner than

memory

faint
-er
    than all the whys
which lurk
between your naked shoulderblades.—Here

comes a stout fellow in a blouse
just outside this window, touching the glass

boxes one by one with his magic
stick(in which a willing

bulb of flame bubbles)
see

here and here they explode
silently into crocuses of brightness. (That is enough
of life, for you. I understand. Once
again. . . .)sliding

a little downward,embrace me with your body's suddenly
curving entire warm questions

THREE sunlight was over
X our mouths fears hearts lungs arms hopes feet hands

under us the unspeaking Mediterranean bluer
than we had imagined
a few cries drifting through
high air
a sail a fishing boat somebody an invisible spectator,
maybe certain nobodies laughing faintly

playing moving far below us

perhaps one villa caught like pieces
of a kite in the trees, here
and here reflecting
sunlight
(everywhere sunlight keen complete
silent

and everywhere you your kisses your flesh mind breathing
beside under around myself)
by and by

a fat colour reared itself against the sky and the sea

. . . finally your eyes knew
me, we smiled to each other, releasing lay, watching
(sprawling, in
grass upon a
cliff) what had been something
else carefully slowly fatally turning into ourselves . . .

while in the very middle of fire all

 the world becoming bright and little melted.

FOUR

FOUR
I

the moon looked into my window
it touched me with its small hands
and with curling infantile
fingers it understood my eyes cheeks mouth
its hands(slipping)felt of my necktie wandered
against my shirt and into my body the
sharp things fingered tinily my heart life

the little hands withdrew, jerkily, themselves
quietly they began playing with a button
the moon smiled she
let go my vest and crept
through the window
she did not fall
she went creeping along the air
                                                                        over houses
                                                                                                roofs

And out of the east toward
her a fragile light bent gatheringly

FOUR
II

if being morticed with a dream
myself speaks

(whispering,
suggesting that our souls
inhabit whatever is between them)
knowing my lips hands the way i move
my habits laughter

i say
you will perhaps pardon,
possibly you will comprehend. and how
this has arrived your mind may guess

if at sunset
it should, leaning against me, smile;
or(between dawn and twilight)giving

your eyes, present me also
with the terror of shrines

which noone has suspected(but
wherein silently
always
are kneeling the various deaths
which are your lover lady: together with what keen
innumerable lives he has not lived.

FOUR
III

here's a little mouse)and
what does he think about, i
wonder as over this
floor(quietly with

bright eyes)drifts(nobody
can tell because
Nobody knows, or why
jerks Here &, here,
gr(oo)ving the room's Silence)this like
a littlest
poem a
(with wee ears and see?

tail frisks)
                    (gonE)
"mouse",
          We are not the same you and

i, since here's a little he
or is
it It
?   (or was something we saw in the mirror)?

therefore we'll kiss;for maybe
what was Disappeared
into ourselves
who   (look).   ,startled

FOUR
IV

but if i should say
goodmorning trouble adds
up all sorts of quickly
things on the slate of that
nigger's
face(but

If i should say thankyouverymuch

mr rosenbloom picks strawberries
with beringed hands)but if

i Should say solong my
tailor
chuckles

like a woman in a dream(but if i
should say
Now the all saucers
but cups if begin to spoons dance every-

should where say over the damned table and we
hold lips Eyes everything
hands you know what
happens)but if i should,
Say,

in spite of everything
which breathes and moves, since Doom
(with white longest hands
neatening each crease)
will smooth entirely our minds

—before leaving my room
i turn, and(stooping
through the morning)kiss
this pillow, dear
where our heads lived and were.

FOUR
VI

you are not going to, dear. You are not going to and
i but that doesn't in the least matter. The big
fear Who held us deeply in His fist is

no longer, can you imagine it
i can't which doesn't matter
and what does is possibly this dear, that we may resume
impact with the inutile collide

once more with the imaginable,love,and eat sunlight(do
you believe it? i begin to and that doesn't matter)which

i suggest teach us a new terror always
which shall brighten
carefully these things we consider life.
Dear i put my eyes into you but that doesn't matter
further than of old

because you fooled the doctors,i touch you with hopes and
words and with so and so: we are together, we will
kiss or smile or move. It's different too isn't it

different dear from moving as we, you
and i,used to move when i thought you were going to(but
that doesn't matter)
when you thought you were going to America.
Then

moving was a matter of not keeping still;we were
two alert lice in the blond hair of nothing

FOUR
VII

since feeling is first
who pays any attention
to the syntax of things
will never wholly kiss you;

wholly to be a fool
while Spring is in the world

my blood approves,
and kisses are a better fate
than wisdom
lady i swear by all flowers. Don't cry
—the best gesture of my brain is less than
your eyelids' flutter which says

we are for each other: then
laugh, leaning back in my arms
for life's not a paragraph

And death i think is no parenthesis

FOUR
VIII

some ask praise of their fellows
but i being otherwise
made compose curves
and yellows, angles or silences
to a less erring end)

myself is sculptor of
your body's idiom:
the musician of your wrists;
the poet who is afraid
only to mistranslate

a rhythm in your hair,
(your fingertips
the way you move)
                                        the

painter of your voice—
beyond these elements

remarkably nothing is. . . . therefore,lady
am i content should any
by me carven thing provoke
your gesture possibly or

any painting(for its own

reason)in your lips
slenderly should create one least smile
(shyly
if a poem should lift to
me the distinct country of your
eyes, gifted with green twilight)

FOUR
IX

supposing i dreamed this)
only imagine, when day has thrilled
you are a house around which
i am a wind—

your walls will not reckon how
strangely my life is curved
since the best he can do
is to peer through windows, unobserved

—listen, for(out of all
things)dream is noone's fool;
if this wind who i am prowls
carefully around this house of you

love being such, or such,
the normal corners of your heart
will never guess how much
my wonderful jealousy is dark

if light should flower:
or laughing sparkle from
the shut house(around and around
which a poor wind will roam

FOUR
X

you are like the snow only
purer fleeter, like the rain
only sweeter frailer you

whom certain
flowers ressemble but trembling(cowards
which fear
to miss within your least gesture the hurting
skill which lives)and since

nothing lingers
beyond a little instant,
along with rhyme and with laughter
O my lady
(and every brittle marvelous breathing thing)

since i and you are on our ways to dust

of your fragility
(but chiefly of your smile,
most suddenly which is
of love and death a marriage)you give me

courage
so that against myself
the sharp days slobber in vain:

Nor am i afraid that
this, which we call autumn, cleverly
dies and over the ripe world wanders with
a near and careful
smile in his mouth(making

everything suddenly old and with his awkward eyes
pushing
sleep under and thoroughly
into all beautiful things)

winter, whom Spring shall kill

FOUR
XI

because
you go away i give roses who
will advise even yourself, lady
in the most certainly(of what we
everywhere do not touch)deep
things;
          remembering ever so
tinily these, your crisp
eyes actually shall contain new faeries

(and if your slim lips are amused, no wisest

painter of fragile
Marys will understand
how smiling may be made as
skilfully.) But carry
also, with that indolent and with
this flower wholly whom you do
not ever fear,
                    me in your heart

softly;not all
but the beginning

of mySelf

you being in love
will tell who softly asks in love,

am i separated from your body smile brain hands merely
to become the jumping puppets of a dream? oh i mean:
entirely having in my careful how
careful arms created this at length
inexcusable, this inexplicable pleasure—you go from several
persons: believe me that strangers arrive
when i have kissed you into a memory
slowly, oh seriously
—that since and if you disappear

solemnly
myselves
ask "life, the question how do i drink dream smile

and how do i prefer this face to another and
why do i weep eat sleep—what does the whole intend"
they wonder. oh and they cry "to be,being,that i am alive
this absurd fraction in its lowest terms
with everything cancelled
but shadows
—what does it all come down to? love? Love
if you like and i like, for the reason that i
hate people and lean out of this window is love,love
and the reason that i laugh and breathe is oh love and the reason

that i do not fall into this street is love."

FOUR
XIII

Nobody wears a yellow
flower in his buttonhole
he is altogether a queer fellow
as young as he is old

when autumn comes,
who twiddles his white thumbs
and frisks down the boulevards

without his coat and hat

—(and i wonder just why that
should please him or i wonder what he does)

and why(at the bottom of this trunk,
under some dirty collars)only a
moment
(or
was it perhaps a year)ago i found staring

me in the face a dead yellow small rose

FOUR
XIV

it is so long since my heart has been with yours

shut by our mingling arms through
a darkness where new lights begin and
increase,
since your mind has walked into
my kiss as a stranger
into the streets and colours of a town—

that i have perhaps forgotten
how, always (from
these hurrying crudities
of blood and flesh) Love
coins His most gradual gesture,

and whittles life to eternity

—after which our separating selves become museums
filled with skilfully stuffed memories

FOUR
XV

i am a beggar always
who begs in your mind

(slightly smiling, patient, unspeaking
with a sign on his
breast
BLIND)yes i

am this person of whom somehow
you are never wholly rid(and who

does not ask for more than
just enough dreams to
live on)
          after all, kid

you might as well
toss him a few thoughts

a little love preferably,
anything which you can't
pass off on other people: for
instance a
plugged promise—

then he will maybe(hearing something
fall into his hat)go wandering
after it with fingers;till having

found
what was thrown away
                              himself
taptaptaps out of your brain, hopes, life

to(carefully turning a
corner)never bother you any more.

FOUR
XVI

if within tonight's erect
everywhere of black muscles fools
a weightless slowness(deftly

muting the world's texture with drifted

gifts of featheriest slenderness and
how gradually which descending are suddenly
received)or by doomfull connivance

accurately thither and hither myself

struts unremembered(rememberingly
with in both pockets curled hands moves)
why then toward morning he is a ghost whom

assault these whispering fists of hail

(and a few windows awaken certain faces
busily horribly blunder through new light
hush we are made of the same thing as perhaps

nothing, he murmurs carefully lying down)

FOUR
XVII

how this uncouth enchanted
person, arising from a
restaurant, looks breathes or moves
—climbing(past light after
light)to turn, disappears

the very swift and
invisibly living
rhythm of your Heart possibly

will understand;
or why(in

this most exquisite of cities)all
of the long night a fragile imitation of
(perhaps)myself carefully wanders
streets dark and, deep

with rain . . . .

(he, slightly whom or
cautiously this person

and this imitation resemble,
descends into the earth with the year
a cigarette between his ghost-lips

gradually)
remembering badly, softly
your
kissed thrice suddenly smile

i go to this window

FOUR
XVIII

just as day dissolves
when it is twilight(and
looking up in fear

i see the new moon
thinner than a hair)

making me feel
how myself has been coarse and dull
compared with you, silently who are
and cling
to my mind always

But now she sharpens and becomes crisper
until i smile with knowing
—and all about
herself

the sprouting largest final air

plunges
            inward with hurled
downward thousands of enormous dreams

FIVE

FIVE
I

after all white horses are in bed

will you walking beside me, my very lady,
if scarcely the somewhat city
wiggles in considerable twilight

touch (now) with a suddenly unsaid

gesture lightly my eyes?
And send life out of me and the night
absolutely into me. . . . a wise
and puerile moving of your arm will
do suddenly that

                                        will do
more than heroes beautifully in shrill
armour colliding on huge blue horses,
and the poets looked at them, and made verses,

through the sharp light cryingly as the knights flew.

FIVE
II

touching you i say (it being Spring
and night) "let us go a very little beyond
the last road—there's something to be found"

and smiling you answer "everything
turns into something else, and slips away....
(these leaves are Thingish with moondrool
and i'm ever so very little afraid")
                                        i say
"along this particular road the moon if you'll
notice follows us like a big yellow dog. You

don't believe? look back. (Along the sand
behind us, a big yellow dog that's .... now it's red
a big red dog that may be owned by who
knows)
        only turn a little your. so. And

there's the moon,there is something faithful and mad"

FIVE
III

along the brittle treacherous bright streets
of memory comes my heart,singing like
an idiot, whispering like a drunken man

who(at a certain corner, suddenly)meets
the tall policeman of my mind.
awake
being not asleep, elsewhere our dreams began
which now are folded: but the year completes
his life as a forgotten prisoner

—"Ici?"—"Ah non, mon cheri; il fait trop froid"—
they are gone: along these gardens moves a wind bringing
rain and leaves, filling the air with fear
and sweetness. . . .pauses. (Halfwhispering. . . .halfsinging

stirs the always smiling chevaux de bois)

when you were in Paris we met here

FIVE
IV

our touching hearts slenderly comprehend
(clinging as fingers, loving one another
gradually into hands) and bend
into the huge disaster of the year:

like this most early single star which tugs

weakly at twilight, caught in thickening fear
our slightly fingering spirits starve and smother;
until autumn abruptly wholly hugs

our dying silent minds, which hand in hand
at some window try to understand
the
(through pale miles of perishing air, haunted
with huddling infinite wishless melancholy,
suddenly looming) accurate undaunted

moon's bright third tumbling slowly

FIVE
V

if i have made, my lady, intricate
imperfect various things chiefly which wrong
your eyes (frailer than most deep dreams are frail)
songs less firm than your body's whitest song
upon my mind—if i have failed to snare
the glance too shy—if through my singing slips
the very skillful strangeness of your smile
the keen primeval silence of your hair

—let the world say "his most wise music stole
nothing from death"—
                                        you only will create
(who are so perfectly alive) my shame:
lady through whose profound and fragile lips
the sweet small clumsy feet of April came

into the ragged meadow of my soul.

Cummings' passionate devotion to individualism is perhaps the most important major theme in his poetry.

the "gang mentality he recognized as a child plus the "gangs" he encountered in his wartime experiences intensified this devotion.

The unique appearance of his poetry is a reflection of the the typographical experimentation his breaking of gramatical rules

<u>Nature</u> — the man who understands and appreciates nature will never lose his individuality or his identity

* he feels children are still in touch with nature — many adults lose their joyfulness and individuality

Cummings' moods are quite virsitile throughout his entire works (romantic, satirical, bitter, humorous) however. However his mood is consistant within one body of work.